Sponsoring C

Second edition

Association for Project Management

Association for Project Management
Ibis House, Regent Park
Summerleys Road, Princes Risborough
Buckinghamshire
HP27 9LE

First edition 2009
Second edition 2018

British Library Cataloguing in Publication Data is available.
Paperback ISBN: 978-1-903494-78-3
eISBN: 978-1-903494-79-0

Cover design by Fountainhead Creative Consultants
Typeset by RefineCatch Limited, Bungay, Suffolk
in 10/14pt Foundry Sans

Contents

Foreword

Sponsors have a misunderstood role; they can create or destroy value for a business. They directly link the corporate direction of the business and project objectives. They determine the value of any business proposal translating these through projects into business-as-usual activities. Being an advocate for the project, they importantly communicate with stakeholder communities with their ever-increasing demands and are accountable for the business benefits delivered through projects. They are the "oil in the business gearbox".

I have seen the importance of the sponsor role at Network Rail, and by developing the role have seen an adjustment in certainty of outcomes, not just meeting key dates, but real benefit delivery. To me a telling observation from the National Audit Office was that "the effectiveness of the project sponsor is the best single predictor of success or failure"; I welcome this document in providing guidance to business leaders in improving the situation.

Sponsoring Change was first published in 2009 and with the evolution of project and business structures has been updated. The two bubble diagrams are the essence of sponsorship – they outline clearly what the sponsor does for the business and for the project. This should be interpreted and applied to businesses involved in any sort of business change, whether hard or soft. Included in the appendices is a helpful list of attributes to consider when choosing a sponsor – this distils what a sponsor is about!

As with the two previous successful publications from the same stable, *Directing Change* and *Governance of Co-Owned Projects*, they apply to all types of organisation and across all sectors. We believe its use will improve governance, bringing greater reward to organisations.

I commend to all business leaders the adoption of this guide.

Mark Carne
Chief executive Network Rail

Acknowledgements

APM wishes to acknowledge the contribution of the following to the content of this guide along with the support of the APM Governance Specific Interest Group (SIG).

Lead Author

Andrew Spiers, Network Rail and deputy chairman Governance SIG

Authors and Contributors

Graham Ball, PwC
Mike Coker, RSPB
Martin Samphire, 3pmxl Ltd and chairman Governance SIG
Danny Trup, Thames Tideway

The authors would also like to thank the following for taking the time to review and comment on drafts of this publication:

Suzanne Davidson
Carol Deveney, Network Rail
Tom Frost, Shell
Roger Garrini, Leonardo
David Hughes, Transport for London
Trevor Jones, DHL
Sue Kershaw, KPMG
Duncan Law, Network Rail
Bill McElroy, Turner & Townsend
Alan Macklin
Andrew Murray, RSM UK
Róisín Naughtan, London Underground
Monica Sasso, Deutsche Bank Group
David Shannon, Oxford Project Management
Natalie Smith
Shaun Thomas, RSPB

1

Purpose

The purpose of this document is to guide board members and senior managers to adopt good practices regarding sponsorship of change projects. Effective sponsorship has been shown to be one of the key factors in delivering change project outcomes successfully.

The guide will help:

- improve understanding of the board's role in applying effective sponsorship of change;
- improve understanding of the role of the project sponsor in governance of any change endeavour;
- develop and improve sponsor competence;
- explain why a sponsor needs to be accountable for project success;
- assure board members, senior managers and others that good sponsorship and robust governance requirements are applied across all projects and programmes managed in their organisation, reduce risks to the organisation and maximise the benefits realised from projects and programmes; and
- ensure that there is a more constructive and productive relationship with those delivering the change project.

2

Introduction

*"The effectiveness of the project sponsor is the best
single predictor of project success or failure"*
NAO annual review of projects – 2015

Organisations spend a significant proportion of their annual budgets on projects, and projects are the primary vehicle for achieving an organisation's strategy. Many of the reasons cited for project failure are linked to the role of the project sponsor. Despite the importance of the role, there has been little guidance for the individual who has been asked to sponsor a project.

This guide has been updated from the original version published in 2009 and explains:

- why every project[1] needs a sponsor;
- how the board's support is important for sponsor and project success;
- the attributes of an effective sponsor that are critical to success;
- what a sponsor does for the business;
- what a sponsor does for a project manager;
- some useful pointers in choosing and selecting a suitable sponsor (Appendix 2).

Sponsors are variously titled, according to practice within their organisations, and may be located at different organisational levels. Whatever a sponsor's level of authority, at a minimum they will be accountable for the project business case, budget, and high-level stakeholder engagement.

---

[1] The terms projects, programmes, project management and programme management are defined in the *APM Body of Knowledge*, and the PMBOK, BS6079. For brevity, this guide uses the term 'project' as being inclusive of project-based programmes and portfolios. Thus, when this guide recommends that every project should have a sponsor, it implies, equally, that every programme and portfolio should have a sponsor.

The programme or project sponsors are accountable for the realisation of desired outcomes and benefits from any investment. They provide the governance link between the organisation's senior executives (the board[2]) and the management of each project.

This APM *Sponsoring Change* guide complements the APM *Directing Change* guide which sets out good practice for the overall governance of enterprise-wide project management and individual projects – one of the core principles being that every project or programme shall have a named and competent sponsor. *Directing Change* also explains the board's responsibility for the overall governance of change and change management across the enterprise and provides checklists for boards and sponsors regarding their governance responsibilities.

The board is accountable for overall sponsorship of the organisational strategy, ensuring a clear line of sight with business-as-usual operations and individual projects and programmes in the organisational portfolio. Clear governance arrangements should be in place for an organisation to undertake any complex change activity. The board is therefore ultimately accountable for ensuring that an appropriate sponsor owns each programme and project and holding them to account for that delegated responsibility, including acting on their behalf in setting the appropriate tone and leadership.

Projects exist to change organisations, their services, performance and/or reputation and impact upon the business to some extent. Business strategy emanates from the board and will guide changes to the business through projects. It is vital to the board that their strategy is turned into reality, confirming the benefits (qualitative and quantitative), understanding the risks and defining boundaries, constraints and dependencies. The board, in setting the agenda for good sponsorship, should consider the important principles described here and ensure they are understood and underwritten.

---

[2] In this guide, the term "board" refers to executive boards, their equivalents in the public sector and to councils in companies limited by guarantee. It does not refer to project boards, which are described separately in section 4 – Organisational context.

Sponsoring Change

Section 6 of this book describes how the sponsor provides accountability, confidence, transparency and understanding to the business, by performing the following advocacy and leadership activities:

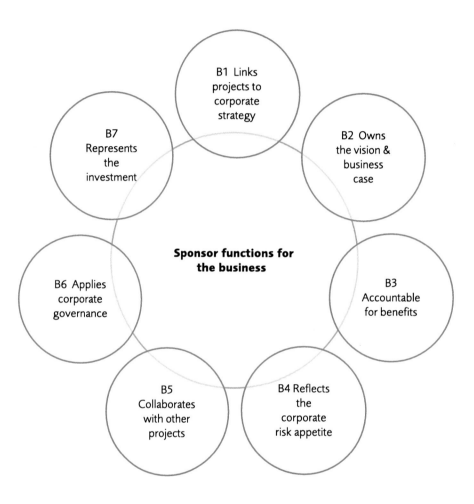

Section 7 describes how the sponsor provides leadership to the project and project manager, and creates the conditions for the project manager and the project team to succeed, by performing the following activities:

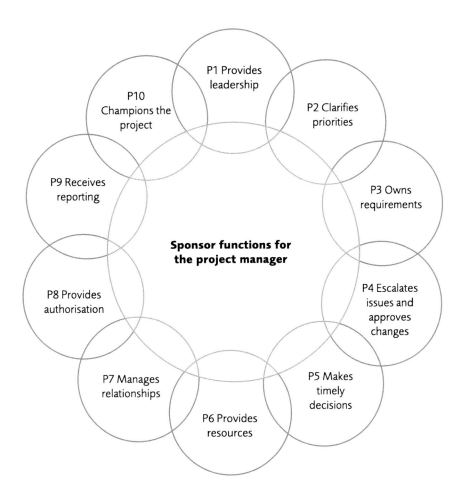

3

Research and reviews

Reports continue to be produced highlighting the failures of high-profile projects, or the poor project delivery success rates in particular sectors. Over the past couple of decades, the focus has shifted from the methods and tools of project delivery, to the people running and leading them. Many reports and academic papers have been written emphasising the importance of effective sponsorship and sponsors in achieving successful project outcomes. Key messages from some of these are outlined below.

APM research in 2015 *Conditions for project success*

> *"the environment in which projects operate and the conditions for project success are at the heart of improving outcomes. And yet, having spoken to over 850 project professionals and thought leaders across the private and public sectors, APM has revealed that while the key to success is known, this practice is often not applied. As a result, nearly 80 per cent of projects fail to wholly meet their planned objectives".*

The study concludes that there are five critical success factors (out of 12) that boards should consider to improve project outcomes:

- **Effective governance:** How do we assure ourselves that the project is where it should be, and who is providing the confidence for us?
- **Goals and objectives (alignment):** Must ensure that corporate strategy and project outcomes are aligned.
- **Capable sponsors:** Have we systems and processes in place to select and support sponsors? Do we have organisational capability?
- **Supportive organisations:** Sponsors should have appropriate organisational support in terms of clear authority, access to decision makers and adequate resources. There should be continuity of sponsorship through the lifecycle and the provision of professional and ethical leadership consistent with its culture and values.

- **End users and operators (stakeholders):** Who is assuring us that the business will accept seamlessly the change and benefits being delivered by the project?

APM *Measures for assuring project success*, published in 2016

This document contains a useful toolkit for business leaders to understand where to concentrate effort in assuring successful project outcomes. Of relevance to sponsorship are the sections:

- **Client[3] and scope:** Clear and controlled baseline requirements, objectives, success criteria, business case, terms of reference, contracts and benefits realisation.
- **Risk and opportunities:** Management of risk and opportunity through the lifecycle of the project.
- **Organisational capability and culture:** People and behaviours.
- **Solution:** The deliverables and outcomes to meet the client requirements.
- **Performance:** Measuring all facets of performance against the baseline requirements, variance analysis and management action.
- **Governance:** The project infrastructure is aligned to corporate structures.

The National Audit Office (NAO) report (January 2016) to the Public Account Select Committee

A key finding was for:

- *"improvements to accountability with greater clarity about the role of SROs[4] (sponsors)".*

Over the past few years, the NAO has observed that project governance, and in effect ownership, has to be strengthened. These observations have come following underperformance on, and failures of, some major projects and programmes. Lessons learned and experience has shown that the appointment

---

[3] The client is the individual or organisation for whom the project outputs are being produced. In some circumstances the client may be the sponsor. See Appendix 1 for more information.
[4] Senior responsible officer/senior responsible owner (SRO) – alternative terms for sponsor.

and empowerment of a sponsor is key to the success of any project, however big or small.

This guide is intended to provide support to sponsors of all sizes of projects. Appendix 1 shows how the sponsor role varies on different types of projects. On even the smallest of projects, the sponsor will be accountable for the project business case, budget, and high-level stakeholder engagement.

4

Organisational context

The establishment of good sponsorship practice is a critical component in an organisation's governance in order to provide support to each sponsor and each project. The board is ultimately accountable for appointing effective sponsors. The sponsor provides the governance link between the organisation's senior executives (the board) and the management of each project.

Directing Change recommends that an organisation's governance should include the governance of project management and identifies project sponsorship as a key component of this process. Project sponsorship authority should therefore be delegated from, and traceable back to, the organisation's board.

Many organisations will be delivering a number of programmes and projects, so the relationship between sponsors, the board and delivery must be clearly expressed and understood. Figure 4.1 shows the generic links that the sponsor has with other key parties. Appendix 1 gives some examples of common variants to this model.

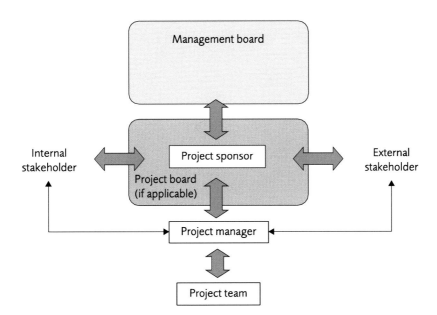

Figure 4.1 Generic governance structure

To the board, the sponsor is accountable for the successful delivery of the project. Working jointly with the project manager, the sponsor defines the project's purpose and objectives, clarifies requirements, takes decisions, provides resources (people, money, etc), garners organisational support and directs the project manager. The sponsor also monitors the project context and leads communications with key stakeholders.

The project sponsor will always remain accountable for the project outcome and may report through some intermediate structure rather than directly to the management board.

5

Successful sponsorship

Success factors are divided into the organisational demands and personal characteristics of a sponsor. Fuller checklists of governance responsibilities for the board and a sponsor are given in *Directing Change, third edition*.

Organisational demands for effective sponsorship

Organisations (and the board) must ensure they always appoint a named sponsor to every project early in its lifecycle and that the sponsor is held accountable for the success of the whole project and its benefits.

A sponsor is the organisational link between the board, senior managers and the project.

The board (and organisation) must provide organisational support for the sponsor and project, and provide an environment and culture that supports the aims of the project at all stages. As sponsors are likely to be busy people, organisational support should include freeing them up from other work so that they can fulfil the role of sponsor.

Organisational support should also include giving the sponsor the level of legitimacy and authority to make appropriate decisions about the project, which may be greater than the legitimacy and authority that comes from the sponsor's position within the organisation.

Personal attributes for a sponsor

The board, in selecting a sponsor, should consider five personal attributes:

- **Understanding**: The sponsor must understand the role, its significance and the project context, risks, etc.
- **Competence:** The sponsor must have the knowledge and skills to fulfil the role. For example, suitable characteristics include strategic view, leadership, collaborative champion, and an understanding of the business case and the needs of the project's client(s).

- **Credibility:** The sponsor must be accepted by stakeholders as suitable for the role via demonstrable experience in the area covered by the project.
- **Commitment**: The sponsor must be able to give the role the personal time and priority necessary to fulfil the duties and responsibilities.
- **Engagement:** The sponsor must be willing to take personal ownership of the project, ensure that effective communications are in place, and be able to influence people toward a successful outcome irrespective of where they sit in the organisation.

These attributes are expanded in the checklist in Appendix 2.

The authors recommend that letters of appointment, or a sponsor brief, should be issued to sponsors clearly setting out their role and how it fits with the organisation's procedures and the context of the particular project that they are sponsoring. Further information on the potential contents of a sponsor brief is included at the end of Appendix 2.

6

What the sponsor does for the business

This section describes how the sponsor provides accountability, confidence, transparency and understanding to the business. Through advocacy and leadership, the sponsor will be the focal point for project success.[5] The sponsor:

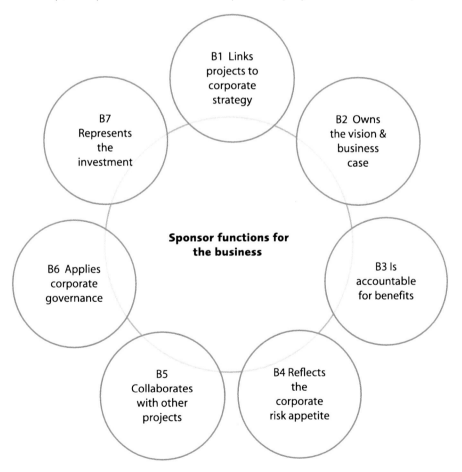

B1 Links projects to corporate strategy

B2 Owns the vision & business case

B3 Is accountable for benefits

B4 Reflects the corporate risk appetite

B5 Collaborates with other projects

B6 Applies corporate governance

B7 Represents the investment

Sponsor functions for the business

[5] As indicated by the generic project structure shown in section 4, the project has internal and external stakeholders, who may include the ultimate client for the project outputs and outcomes.

B1 Links projects to corporate strategy

Projects deliver or enable the strategy of their business. The sponsor understands how project outputs and benefits contribute to strategic objectives and organisational success. That understanding is at the core of decisions taken by the sponsor and informs negotiation with third parties.

Alignment between projects and strategy should be clear in the documents that define the business case, vision, requirements and objectives. The sponsor should also identify and articulate how success will be measured.

An informed sponsor understands how changes in corporate strategy influence objectives and the continuing validity of the project. This is vital for decisions to be made in a timely and informed manner. The sponsor provides the conduit by which corporate decisions are cascaded to project teams.

The sponsor should also be able to recognise any opportunities to increase the return on investment of the project, and create the confidence in the board to act decisively on those opportunities within the bounds of affordability.

It is particularly important to ensure that corporate ethics and culture are not inadvertently distorted or changed by project teams. The sponsor represents the board to the project and vice versa to mitigate this risk.

B2 Owns the vision and business case

The vision and project business case is the core justification by which the board should be satisfied of the value of investing in the project.

The sponsor oversees the production and approval of the project business case, and is responsible for its maintenance throughout the life of the project. The business case should reflect the corporate appetite for risk and contain projections of future business performance. The sponsor should understand in some detail the construction and tolerances within the case for investment.

The sponsor should be able to articulate the overall (compelling) vision, key costs, benefits and business drivers which create the business case and should understand the degree of change that the business case can viably tolerate and should understand how these factors are prioritised and connected to support board decisions, particularly in complex or competitive investment environments. These factors will also help clarify the scope of the project and the options for its delivery.

The sponsor establishes the success criteria for the project through consultation with the board, key stakeholders and the project manager. Assumptions, dependencies and constraints should be challenged, where necessary, to ensure that the business case is realistic and stakeholder expectations are appropriate.

To achieve this, the sponsor must provide visibility of the project beyond the immediate timescales of delivery. The sponsor must understand how costs are offset by the accumulation of benefits once the project has delivered its outputs and ensure a smooth transition to those who will realise the project's benefits.

B3 Is accountable for benefits

The sponsor is accountable, to the board, for the whole project including both delivery success and realisation of the benefits. Hence, the sponsor must understand how benefits are derived, valued and measured. The sponsor is also accountable for assessing how changes to the project impact benefits and hence project viability, and reporting that position to the board as required.

The sponsor should place the realisation of desired benefits at the core of delivery aligning them to corporate goals or objectives. This accountability is retained by the sponsor throughout the project lifecycle and beyond project close.

Responsibility for benefits realisation may be formally delegated or transferred to other owners/users post project completion. However, the sponsor remains accountable for the overall long-term success of the investment.

B4 Reflects the corporate risk appetite

The sponsor promotes compliance with mandated corporate risk procedures, and cascades the corporate tolerance for risk into the planning of the project. A critical part of this is to make sure that the project is not exposing the organisation to a higher level of risk than the organisation is prepared to bear. Projects may be subject to intensive scrutiny by the board when their delivery is more likely to influence the success or viability of the parent organisation. The sponsor should encourage the project team to be proactive in the identification and management of risks and opportunities in a fully transparent manner. The sponsor should make sure that the project team has the capabilities needed to manage delivery risks.

The sponsor is accountable for overseeing the management of outcome risk[6] throughout the project. This should be consistent with the organisation's approach to project assurance, which should cover risks to the delivery of the project that impact the business case, risks to the organisation caused by the project (e.g. reputation), impact of the project on stakeholders and the organisation's operating environment and where necessary ensuring that risks are promptly escalated to the board for response. The sponsor should help the project team ensure risks to the organisation are being appropriately mitigated through the project and, at the end of the project, transfer outcome risks to the client.

B5 Collaborates with other projects

Organisations often develop many projects in parallel. The sponsor provides the principal point of business interface between a project and the organisation's wider portfolio. This is a vital role if the organisation's portfolio is to be delivered in a coherent, controlled and optimal manner.

The management of risk across the organisation's portfolio is the responsibility of the board, or an appropriate body that responsibility has been delegated to such as a portfolio board. The sponsor should proactively collaborate with other sponsors to achieve their collective business cases. The board should be encouraging all sponsors to recognise the compound effects of all of these changes and/or dependencies and optimise the timeline and impact of their specific project accordingly.

B6 Applies corporate governance

The sponsor assures that corporate governance arrangements and policies (and any third-party governance requirements) are being applied on behalf of the board. If the project is being managed in phases or stages, then the sponsor may authorise progress through gates subject to the organisation's agreed procedures. Unless mandated otherwise by the organisation's procedures, the sponsor will be responsible for determining when and how to engage independent assessors[7] and then coordinate their involvement.

---

[6] The residual risk to the organisation, or the maintenance of the outputs, once the project has completed

[7] In some organisations this role is performed by the Project Management Office (PMO) or equivalent

The sponsor assures that his/her project is delivered in compliance with corporate policies and procedures, and that roles and responsibilities for governance on the project are clearly defined and allocated.

The sponsor assures that formal methodology, processes and disciplined governance arrangements, supported by appropriate ethics, cultures, policies, methods, resources and controls, are applied throughout the programme and project life cycle as designated by the organisation. Where there is non-adherence to corporate standards, a justification shall be agreed with the board.

The sponsor ensures the project is formally started and closed at the appropriate time.

If the outputs of a project are going to be handed to a third party, then the sponsor must understand their governance arrangements and ensure that they are appropriately reflected in the acceptance criteria for the project outputs.

The sponsor ensures that appropriate lessons from other projects are embedded into his/her project and that lessons are shared openly with other projects.

B7 Represents the investment

It is the sponsor's role to ensure that the project is represented, and the business case for the investment is understood at senior stakeholder forums in order to promote rational and informed decisions. This may typically include representation of the project to periodic review panels and stakeholder groups at which progress will be reported and key decisions agreed.

The sponsor may also represent both project and business interests to third parties, securing the approvals, terms or negotiated outcomes that serve both delivery and business requirements.

The sponsor can also present decisions made within the project to review forums to promote understanding and agreement with the stakeholders in the senior management community.

The sponsor may have to promote the project to senior governance panels and should provide confidence to the board and senior stakeholders that a coherent and reliable plan for delivery has been established, that progress is appropriate, that suitable action is being taken to manage issues, that formal change management is in place, and that the benefits of the investment will be realised.

7

What the sponsor does for the project manager

This section describes how the sponsor provides leadership to the project and project manager, and creates the conditions for the project manager and the project team to succeed. The project sponsor:

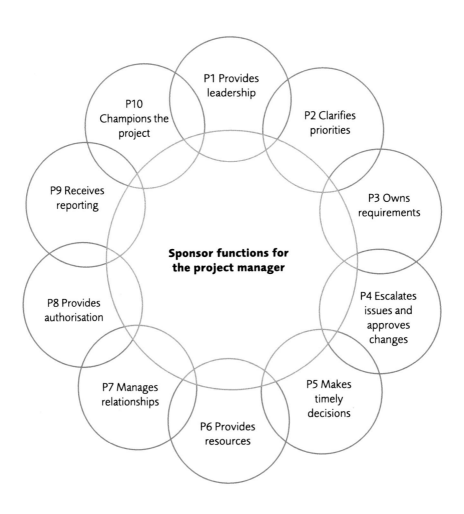

P1 Provides leadership

P2 Clarifies priorities

P3 Owns requirements

P4 Escalates issues and approves changes

P5 Makes timely decisions

P6 Provides resources

P7 Manages relationships

P8 Provides authorisation

P9 Receives reporting

P10 Champions the project

Sponsor functions for the project manager

P1 Provides leadership

The sponsor operates in a leadership role, providing instruction, guidance and representation of the organisation and board to the project manager and senior stakeholders. The role should be complementary to and support the project manager to achieve the desired project and business outcome(s).

The sponsor should complement the delivery focus of the project manager with organisational and contextual awareness and foresight. The sponsor should make sure that the project remains achievable and should encourage the project manager to look for efficiencies and identify opportunities to improve the business case. If the project's business case is no longer achievable, then the sponsor should ensure that appropriate action is taken. Actions under consideration should include project termination.

The sponsor should support the project using their wider influence within the organisation. If project recovery action is required, the sponsor will provide appropriate challenge of the project plans, assess business-case impacts and provide support (as appropriate) to build confidence with affected stakeholders, reporting key messages to the board as necessary.

The sponsor should be a 'critical friend' of the project manager providing both motivation and challenge as necessary. It is likely that the sponsor will have an active role in the project manager's performance assessments.

The sponsor ensures that the project is managed in a way that is consistent with the culture and values of the organisation. The sponsor sets expectations of ethics, quality, transparency and challenge, creating an environment in which decisions made about the project are taken using realistic information on forecasts and progress.

P2 Clarifies priorities

The sponsor provides the project manager with the vision, business case, outcomes, requirements and anticipated benefits of the project. The sponsor should help the project manager understand and interpret this information in order to allow appropriate focus in delivery and facilitate trade-offs when constraints influence delivery and hence the business case outcome. The sponsor will need to understand the relative priorities of the project outputs and outcomes, and the requirements associated with these outputs and outcomes. The sponsor will work closely with the project manager to determine how these output, outcome and requirement priorities are reflected in the respective priorities of the packages of work making up the project.

P3 Owns requirements

The sponsor defines what success looks like and owns the requirements against which the project must deliver. These requirements should reflect the outcomes to be achieved, any specifications to which the project's solution must comply, as well as recommendations to be evaluated. The sponsor should be confident that the outputs, produced to meet these requirements, will serve the business case and be acceptable to the end user of that output. The sponsor may have to negotiate compromises between conflicting requirements and remove any ambiguity perceived by the delivery team to safeguard intended outcomes. The sponsor also needs to ensure the project manager fully understands the requirements, the acceptable level of tolerances with respect to output quality and timing, and delivery risks.

P4 Escalates issues and approves changes

The sponsor is the escalation route for any issues that the project manager and project team are not able to deal with. The sponsor ensures prompt escalation to the appropriate governance level, and champions the resolution of appropriate issues.

Where proposed changes to the project have the potential to impact upon requirements or outputs, or where the support of third parties or the board is required to implement a change, the sponsor should be consulted and play a key role in negotiating an agreeable position.

The sponsor keeps the project manager informed of matters relating to board and stakeholder decisions which could have an impact on the success of the project and takes responsibility for actions that require senior management commitment.

The sponsor is also responsible for supporting the project manager to make sure that all significant changes to the scope of the project are managed through an appropriate auditable change process, ensuring that approved changes don't undermine the project's business case.

P5 Makes timely decisions

The sponsor should clarify the criteria and processes to be used to escalate issues and risks to the board. Too much escalation will undermine the project manager's authority, whilst failure to escalate could make the sponsor ineffective and put undue risk on the business case. Appropriately defined escalation criteria facilitate timely decisions, ensure effective implementation, and allow the sponsor to create confidence in the project.

Where a sponsor is given delegated authority to make decisions on behalf of the board, these should be made in a timely manner and with due consideration of the business case, benefits, requirements, deliverability and cost. Delays in decisions can be a major cause of project delays, and frustration within the project team. The sponsor needs to be aware of this and act to ensure decision making is timely.

Where other bodies are required to make decisions on behalf of the project, the sponsor should lead the escalation.

P6 Provides resources

The sponsor should interpret requests for resources from the project manager and ensure that reasonable requests are met whilst maintaining an appropriate level of return on investment in line with the business case. This may include approval of new funding and/or extra purchasing requests.

The sponsor may also play a role in making sure that non-financial resources, such as staff and other assets, are made available as required by the project manager. This may require the sponsor to work with other stakeholders to ensure that they support the delivery of the project and to help them find solutions when their own resource constraints endanger project success.

Note that the sponsor is an important project resource and should make sure that they have the time and the capabilities to provide the support that the project manager needs.

The sponsor should ensure that the project team has the necessary delegated authority, resources, competencies, tools, capability and culture to succeed.

P7 Manages relationships

The sponsor personally develops relationships with those senior stakeholders who may influence delivery, or be the eventual owners of the outputs of the project. These may be internal or external to the sponsor's organisation. The sponsor uses these relationships to communicate the project's objectives, benefits, and requirements, and systematically communicates output from these relationships to the project manager, and champions relationship development across the project.

   The sponsor should ensure all stakeholders are engaged proportionately and honestly, commensurate with their interest, effect on the outcome of the project and how they are impacted, in a manner that fosters understanding and trust.

P8 Provides authorisation

If the project is being managed in phases or stages, then the sponsor may authorise progress through gates subject to the organisation's agreed procedures. At the appropriate stage gates, or checkpoints, the project manager should present the status of the project for review and challenge, prior to authorisation or recommendation from the sponsor.

   The sponsor may approve the progression of the project and attach conditions which should be completed by the project within defined timescales and delegated authority. Conditional approval is an important mechanism for the sponsor to maintain project momentum whilst mitigating the risk of projects progressing through a gate before all the necessary conditions have been met. Depending on the organisation's procedures, stage-gate reviews or checkpoints may require independent assessors.

   Where the project forms part of a wider portfolio or programme, the sponsor will decide and agree with the project manager what level of engagement the stage gate review or checkpoint requires.

P9 Receives reporting

The sponsor should receive regular progress reports with agreed metrics on the performance of the project and should be able to provide constructive challenge to the project team. Using their experience and expertise, sponsors should be able to identify key challenges, threats and opportunities and help the project to respond accordingly. The sponsor should be honest about whether or not they have the skills and experience to provide this challenge, for this type of project. If they don't have the skills or experience, the sponsor should seek support from outside the project team so that they can get independent advice and hence provide insightful challenge.

Effective reporting will also assist the sponsor in representing the performance of the project to more senior stakeholders.

P10 Champions the project

The sponsor must act as the champion for the project and its context to ensure organisational and external support for the project. This involves ensuring good collaboration with external suppliers and stakeholders, external approval bodies, board members, and operational departments, etc.

The sponsor should work with the project manager to ensure that the project team have the necessary conditions[8] for success and have learnt from previous successes and failures. This should include understanding how to motivate and reward the team, encouraging them to learn throughout the project, and (depending upon the organisation) making sure that there is a plan for what happens to the project team members when the project finishes.

The sponsor should also ensure that the project team are sharing their lessons learned with the rest of the organisation during and at the end of the project.

---

[8] Project team culture is a key condition for success in some organisations. For example, in an organisation with a poor track record of project delivery, the sponsor may need to actively create a different culture in the project team from that in the wider organisation.

Appendix 1

Alternative governance structures

Projects and programmes

In project management terminology, a programme refers to a group of related projects. This guide uses the word project to refer to both projects and programmes. **This guide recommends that each programme and each of its constituent projects should have a sponsor**. These will usually be different people.

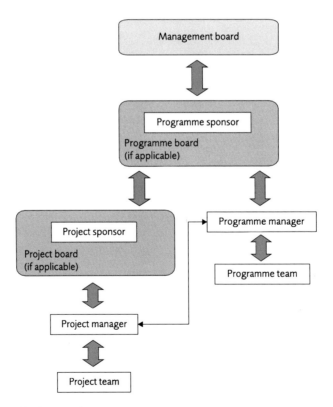

Figure A.1 Project and programme governance structure

Projects, programmes and portfolios

The organisation may organise its projects and programmes into one or more portfolios in order to optimise the deployment of resources. One possible structure is shown in Figure A.2 where the project (or programme) sponsor is accountable to a portfolio. The portfolio could be directly governed by the main board or could have its own portfolio board.

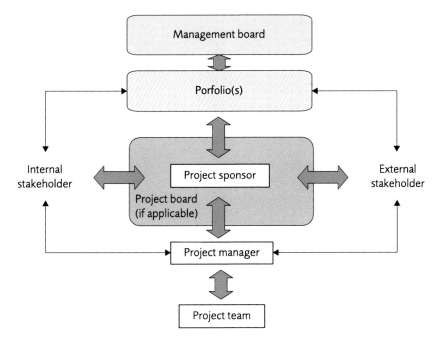

Figure A.2 Portfolio governance structure

Multi-organisational projects

Many projects involve more than one organisation. Examples include projects that involve client–contractor relationships and projects that are reliant on the contribution of multiple organisations. In these circumstances, each organisation should regard its contribution as a project in its own right and be able to identify the person who fulfils their project sponsor's role. It should also be made clear which organisation has overall ownership of the project and how disputes between the organisations will be resolved if the respective project sponsors are not able to resolve them.

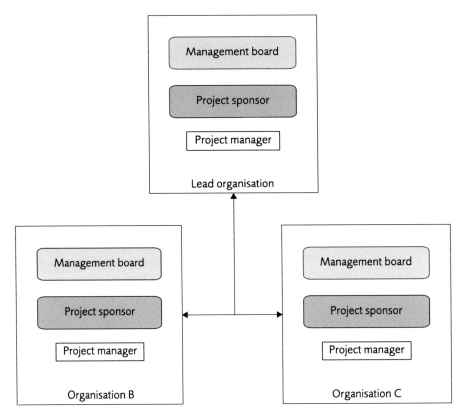

Figure A.3 Multi-organisational governance structure

Trustee-led organisations

In certain organisations, such as charities, the organisation's trustees provide an additional level of governance. In the charity sector, regulation makes the trustees accountable for certain aspects of the organisation's work. As these include aspects of project and programme delivery, consideration has to be given to how the project sponsor will represent the trustees. In some circumstances, a trustee could be the project sponsor, or the project sponsor could report to a trustee (or trustees) rather than the board.

Agile projects and programmes

Agile is an umbrella term for a range of project delivery techniques where cost and time are usually fixed, but quality (scope/benefits) can be varied to meet cost and time constraints. Agile can be used as a stand-alone project management methodology or can be used alongside more traditional linear methodologies within the project. From a governance perspective, the key difference is that in an agile approach decisions about the scope of the project are taken at the time required by the project and not at pre-defined times (e.g. at project boards). Hence, decision making is delegated to the project team, and the sponsor must be an active member of that team.

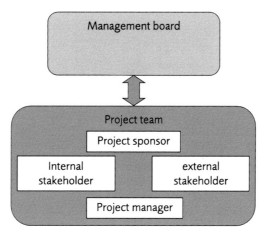

Figure A.4 Agile governance

The APM publication *Directing Agile Change* provides more information on the sponsorship of agile projects.

Business change managers

Some project and programme management methodologies have additional roles reporting into the sponsor. In this situation, it is important to clarify what the additional role(s) are responsible for and hence what impact this has on the role of the sponsor, and their relationship with the project manager. For example, in some methodologies, benefits realisation is split from the project manager role and becomes the responsibility of one or more business change managers who also report to the sponsor.

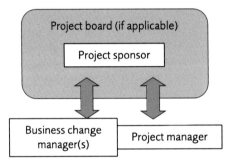

Figure A.5 Business change manager(s)

Appendix 2

Choosing a sponsor

The following lists expand upon the five personal attributes identified in section 5.

Understanding
- Understands the organisation's governance arrangements
- Understands the sponsorship role
- Understands the project context
- Appreciates how the project contributes to the corporate strategy

Competence
- Provides clarity of direction
- Identifies and focuses on what matters most
- Manages people and other resources effectively
- Makes effective decisions and takes decisive action when necessary
- Motivates people
- Negotiates effectively
- Has relevant experience
- Has sufficient appreciation of the project's technical requirements
- Has a good understanding of project management
- Self-aware about strengths and weaknesses
- Demonstrates good judgement
- Commercial awareness of risk
- Strategic risk management
- Value management

Credibility
- Respected by major stakeholders
- Ability to influence internal and external stakeholders
- Evident track record
- Motivated to act in the long-term interest of the organisation

Sponsoring Change

Commitment
- ☐ Has time to commit to project outcomes, short and long term

Engagement
- ☐ Has other responsibilities within the organisation that gives insight into its dynamics
- ☐ Aligns the project with the interests of the organisation
- ☐ Obtains regular updates on the organisation's strategy

Letters of appointment, or a sponsor brief, should be issued to sponsors clearly setting out their accountability, stating the point at which they become accountable for the project, and defining the tenure of the role linked to key milestones. The letter of appointment, or sponsor brief, should summarise the reason for the project, the sponsor's assurance responsibilities, if and how the project does not need to adhere to organisational standards, and what will happen if the sponsor leaves before the project is completed. This will lead to a more stable environment for sponsors to exercise their duties and, crucially, they are recognised as such and supported at the very highest level.

Directing Change provides additional checklists for the sponsor role against the five components of effective governance:

- portfolio direction and alignment;
- programme and project sponsorship;
- change and project, programme and portfolio management capability;
- transparency and assurance;
- culture and ethics.

Appendix 3

Glossary of key terms

Ref	Name	Definition	Source
1	Assurance	P3 Assurance is the process of providing confidence to stakeholders that projects, programmes and portfolios will achieve their scope, time, cost and quality objectives and realise their benefits	*APM Body of Knowledge* 3.6.1 P3 Assurance
2	Board	The organisation's management board (not project board). The role of an organisation's board can be summarised as: ■ providing entrepreneurial leadership; ■ setting strategy (and sponsoring the change portfolio); ■ ensuring the human and financial resources are available to achieve objectives; ■ reviewing management performance; ■ setting the company's values and standards; ■ ensuring that obligations to shareholders and other stakeholders are understood and met	*UK Corporate Governance Code*
3	Change initiatives	A change initiative is a structured and complex endeavour moving an organisation from the current state to the desired future state. An initiative may be one component of the organisation's vision and strategic plan for the future	
4	Change management	The structured management approach involved in organising and controlling change initiatives	*APM Body of Knowledge Glossary*: change management
5	Culture	The set of shared values and norms that characterise a particular organisation or part thereof. Values can resonate with employees' higher ideals and rally them around a set of meaningful goals. They also focus employees' attention on organisational priorities, which then guide their behaviour and decision-making. Organisational culture can limit the scope for strategic change	Adapted from ft.com/lexicon

6	Ethics	Moral rules or principles of behaviour that should guide members of a profession or organisation and make them deal honestly and fairly with each other and with their customers	Adapted from ft.com/lexicon, from *Longman Business English Dictionary*
7	Corporate governance	Corporate governance involves a set of relationships between a company's management, its board, its shareholders and other stakeholders. Corporate governance also provides the structure through which the objectives of the company are set, and the means of attaining those objectives and monitoring performance are determined	OECD definition: *OECD Principles of Corporate Governance 2015*
8	Portfolio	A grouping of an organisation's change initiatives, projects and programmes. Portfolios can be managed at an organisational or functional level	*APM Body of Knowledge Glossary*: Portfolio
9	Portfolio alignment	Clear and visible alignment of the portfolio to the organisation's strategy which will allow prioritisation and promote the resolution of conflict	Adapted from *APM Body of Knowledge* Ch 2: People
10	Programme	A group of related projects and change activities that together achieve beneficial change for an organisation	*APM Body of Knowledge Glossary*: Programme
11	Project	A unique, transient endeavour undertaken to achieve planned objectives	*APM Body of Knowledge Glossary*: Project
12	Project board	The project board is responsible for supporting the sponsor to provide the overall direction, oversight and management of the project within the constraints set out by the organisation's board. It is accountable for the success of the project under the chairmanship of the sponsor	Adapted from *Managing Successful Projects with PRINCE2* (2009): Organization p33
13	Project manager	The person given the authority and responsibility to manage a project on a day-to-day basis to deliver the required products within the constraints agreed with the sponsors and project board	*Managing Successful Projects with PRINCE2* (2009) Glossary: Project Manager

14	Sponsor	The sponsor is accountable for the realisation of desired outcomes and benefits from any investment or initiative. S/he provides the governance link between the organisation's senior executives (the board) and the management of each project. They provide the primary challenge to the project manager and link corporate direction and accountability with projects – they are responsible for the effective governance of their projects and the overall business case and are also responsible for establishing and monitoring the culture and ethics of the project	*APM Body of Knowledge Glossary*: adapted from *Sponsoring Change*
15	Transparency	Officials, managers, board members and businessmen act openly and unambiguously communicate their activities, and can be held accountable for their actions.	Adapted from Transparency International's definition

Appendix 4

References and further reading

APM (2012) *APM Body of Knowledge 6th edition*. UK

APM (2014) *Guide to Integrated Assurance. UK*

APM (2015) *Conditions for Project Success*. UK

APM (2016) *Directing Agile Change. UK*

APM (2016) *Governance of Co-Owned Projects*. UK

APM (2016) *Introduction to Programme Management. UK*

APM (2017) *Introduction to Managing Change. UK*

APM (2018) *Directing Change, 3rd edition. UK*

Axelos (2007) *Management of Portfolios (MoP®)*. UK

Axelos (2007) *Managing Successful Programmes (MSP®)*. UK

Axelos (2009) PRINCE2® – **PR**ojects **IN C**ontrolled **E**nvironments. UK

Agile Business Consortium / DSDM (2014) *Agile Project Management Framework*. UK

Agile Business Consortium / DSDM (2014) *Agile Programme Management Framework*. UK

Parliament of the United Kingdom (2016) UK Companies Act. UK

ISO 21505 (2017) *Project, programme and portfolio management – Guidance on Governance*. EU

BS 6079-1 (2010) *Principles and guidelines for the management of projects*

ICE – Infrastructure Client Group (2017) – A new approach to delivering high performing infrastructure – Project 13. UK